PROSPECTING MADE EASY

It's just _NOT_ that hard!

Robert E. Krumroy, CLU, ChFC

Prospecting Made Easy. It's just NOT that hard!

©2011 by Robert E. Krumroy

Publish date: October 2011

Given the current legal environment, we suggest that you consult your compliance or legal advisors before adapting the ideas presented in this book. We have not intentionally included any advice or materials that put you at risk, but we also realize how quickly and often laws and regulations change regarding the financial services industry.

This book is for general information purposes. The author of this material is independent and unaffiliated with any financial service company. Your company's compliance policies, procedures and initiatives will govern over any marketing strategies presented in this book that deviate from them.

Before any ideas are implemented, all correspondence and materials used with prospects or clients must be compliance-approved. The terms "advisor," "agent," "professional" and "representative" may appear in this book. Your company may consider that these different titles signify different capacities and roles. Please check with your compliance department for appropriate terminology when using any of these terms in printed format. Additionally, before making a telephone call to a prospect, make sure you are in compliance with your company procedures and the federal regulations pertaining to Do Not Call.

I-B Publishing, Greensboro, NC

ISBN: 978-0-9678661-9-2

Layout & Design by Jerry Odom

"A successful career is built on a lifelong commitment to effective prospecting. This book provides a back-to-basics approach to effective prospecting tips and scripts for any producer. Krumroy makes it simple!"

Dayton H. Molendorp
CLU, Chairman, President and CEO
ONEAMERICA

"Krumroy, the master of relationship-based marketing, illustrates why every prospect will be someone's client in the future. Why not yours? They will be if you follow the principles in this book. Read the book and discover why prospecting is really NOT that hard!"

Jeffrey R. Hughes
CEO
GAMA INTERNATIONAL

"The material is field tested by a great field leader, trainer, and teacher and can be applied as soon as you read it. Prospecting Made Easy is now in every new agent tool kit and in the hands of all licensed staff that have prospecting responsibilities."

Ken Gallacher
FSS, CLF, LUTCF, Regional Director Pacific Intermountain Region
AMERICAN NATIONAL

"For the last 22 years of training agents, this is one of the most practical books that I have read with ready-to-use applications. The strategies help agents create attraction to their business, which ultimately helps them create large, profitable books of business."

Thresa Cochran
CLU, ChFC, CLF
AMERICAN NATIONAL

"Best prospecting book in the industry! Krumroy hits it out of the park. Give this book to every agent. It's a must read."

William D. Pollakov
CLU, ChFC, President and CEO
THE POLLAKOV FINANCIAL GROUP,
A GENERAL AGENCY OF MASSMUTUAL FINANCIAL GROUP

Additional endorsements on pages 64–65

About the Author

Robert E. Krumroy

CEO, author of eight books and founder of Identity Branding, Inc. and e-Relationship, has been teaching the principles of prospect attraction to financial sales professionals for more than 30 years. His impressive career placed him among the top 100 financial managers in the financial industry. Referred to as The Prospect-Attraction Coach, Robert is a nationally recognized speaker and teacher. The powerful strategy he teaches has dramatically improved sales, prospect access, retention and recruiting for many of the leading financial service companies in the U.S. He lives in Greensboro, NC.

Table of Contents

THE POINT IX
The 12 Most Frequently Asked Questions about Prospecting
Answers to the 12 Most Frequently Asked Questions about Prospecting
The 4 Sources for Prospects

PREFACE XXI

CHAPTER ONE 1
Rethinking Prospecting

CHAPTER TWO 5
Never Lose a Prospect. It's a Future CLIENT!

CHAPTER THREE 9
From Prospect to Easy Appointment
Getting Started with Luggage Tags

CHAPTER FOUR 17
Transitioning Friends to Easy Appointments

CHAPTER FIVE 21
Embracing My Natural Market

CHAPTER SIX 29
What Are the Best Target Markets?

CHAPTER SEVEN 37
Event Prospecting

CHAPTER EIGHT 45
Making a Lifetime Career Commitment to Prospecting

CHAPTER NINE 49
Social Media – Image Enhancement, Sales, Referrals

EPILOGUE 53

ADVISOR TOOLBOX 55

THE
POINT

New and experienced advisors alike know that getting prospects to agree to an appointment is difficult — more difficult than ever before. What changed? Prospecting used to be quite simple. Only a few years ago prospecting was the simple art of finding people who needed your product and could afford to pay for it. After that, your job was to bravely call an adequate number of these people and persuade them to meet with you.

It worked then, but something has changed.

Today, most people require more than just knowing you casually or meeting you once or twice before agreeing to an appointment to discuss financial issues. When prospects haven't experienced anything that is relevantly unique about you within your profession, most aren't willing to exchange valuable time for what they anticipate will be another same-old financial encounter. They need to experience something that separates you from the competition, something that delivers a compelling attraction and initiates a meaningful connection. More often than not, this skill is overlooked or misunderstood, and the results are apparent — more than 87% of financial advisors meet with failure due to their inability to secure adequate appointments (Source: LIMRA, *Agent Production and Retention Report 2009*, Executive Summary).

Any advisor can easily identify a few hundred prospects within his or her church, civic club or social network. Failure isn't the result of an inability to identify hundreds of prospects, or having a bad phone script, or poor sales training. Failure is due to getting too few appointments. In summary, it's **_all_** about prospecting — the skill of creating a compelling and unique attraction that turns prospects into appointments.

If you want superior career retention and production, it's time to get a grip on the real skill: prospecting ... or should I say *real prospecting!* There's a big difference.

The 12 Most Frequently Asked Questions about Prospecting

1: Do you believe that every prospect is a future client?

2: Why is prospecting the most important skill for both new and experienced advisors?

3: Is target marketing the same as prospecting?

4: Do most experienced advisors have prospecting problems?

5: Should an advisor's clients be part of a prospect database?

6: What's more important: getting referrals or prospecting?

7: Why doesn't the insurance industry spend more time emphasizing prospecting?

8: Does a growing prospect database increase sales for experienced agents?

9: How can I get day-to-day acquaintances and social contacts, whether at my church or other organizations where I am involved, to agree to an appointment?

10: Are demographic segments often confused as target markets?

11: Do advisors often mistake having a product focus as a target market?

12: Are some groups too loosely connected to be good target markets?

Answers to the 12 Most Frequently Asked Questions about Prospecting

1: Do you believe that every prospect is a future client? You should. The facts are on your side! Almost eight in ten American households currently do not have a personal life insurance agent and most of them say they never did. That's not surprising considering that 71% of newly contracted agents leave the business within their first two calendar years. Additionally, half of U.S. households (58 million) and 33% of affluent households ($100,000+ income) say they need more life insurance and one in four households plan to buy life insurance for themselves or another household member in the next 12 months (Source: LIMRA, *2010 Life Insurance Ownership Study*). You should assume that every prospect is going to buy something that you offer in the next ten years. The question is, will it be from you, or the competition? The answer will be more influenced by your ongoing connection with your prospect than any other single component.

When you decide that every prospect is a future client, the value of prospecting climbs dramatically. Every advisor can add fifteen new prospects each month to a database by just paying attention and making it a serious commitment. Social contacts, new friends, referrals and organizations are all constant sources of new prospects. Fifteen new prospects this month means fifteen new clients in the future, if you stay connected.

When you build a prospect database and begin connecting regularly, you almost instantly become everyone's second-favorite financial professional and you're not far from being #1. Start making connections. Never lose a prospect. Every one of them will eventually become a new client.

2: Why is prospecting the most important skill for both new and experienced advisors? The skill of prospecting has traditionally been taught as the ability to identify people who need your product and can more than likely afford it. Today, that definition is inadequate. We all know failed advisors and mediocre producers who are acquainted with hundreds of people through church, civic groups or charity work, by serving on boards, or in the general community, but they can't get the appointment. Why? Because most people require more than just knowing you're in the business before they will agree to an appointment. Most people need to see a unique identifier, something that creates market separation for you, as compared to what they regard as typical in your industry. Without a unique identifier, there is little reason to agree to an appointment.

3: Is target marketing the same as prospecting? Not totally. Consider the following analogy. During the early years of settling America, it was well known that locating the buffalo herd was not the totality of buffalo hunting. To be successful, engaging the buffalo herd required an effective approach and timing strategy. Similarly, target marketing is not just about finding a group of prospects you can drop in on each month, meet a few new people and then call for appointments the next day. That's ambushing, not marketing.

Target marketing is more than selecting a group to get prospects from; it is about selecting a group or groups that you are willing to give value to. Your starting point is to find a group of people that needs your product, appreciates each other, has a common cause, and meets regularly. But high-level success requires getting visibly involved and having a strategy that builds compelling attraction and approachability. The greatest target marketing success stories are from agents who make a lifetime career commitment to a specific group or groups, get intimately involved, deliver visible value, and build their reputation and approachability.

4: Do most experienced advisors have prospecting problems? Yes. Many advisors depend on current clients, a few referrals and an occasional new social contact to produce a good year. They all have twenty-five or fifty prospect names in their heads that they would love to engage in an appointment, but they can't. They know the answer to an appointment request would be a "no." That is a prospecting problem.

5: Should an advisor's clients be part of a prospect database? If you don't categorize your prospects apart from your clients, it's easy to think you're actively prospecting when you're not. Most experienced advisors will boast about the size of their database until asked to subtract the number of clients from it and identify only those who are prospects — a number that is nearly always fewer than fifty.

This means there is little focus on strategic prospecting aimed at building prospect approachability and delivering their reputation. If advisors don't have separate or categorized prospect databases, they usually have far fewer prospects than they think. Existing clients may be the logical place to find cross-selling opportunities, but even senior advisors want a certain number of new clients each year. Without a separate prospect database, we find there isn't much attention given to prospecting and most senior advisors experience a diminishing number of new client sales.

6: **What's more important: getting referrals or prospecting?** Both! That's like asking whether gas or shock absorbers are more important to a car. Gas is what gets the car to go — without enough of it, your journey will end prematurely. Shock absorbers give you a smooth ride — without them, you won't enjoy the journey. You have to pay attention to both; your level of gas (prospecting) and the presence of shock absorbers (referrals) are both critical to your career.

7: **Why doesn't the insurance industry spend more time emphasizing prospecting?** Until a few short years ago, there were plenty of prospects. New agent training focused primarily on selling. The industry believed that prospecting was about being brave, resilient, gregarious and outgoing, along with making enough phone calls to fill your appointment calendar. It is no longer that simple. "Do-not-call," people getting information from the Internet, lack of trust, and a myriad of other reasons have made prospecting a priority once again. Failures aren't happening because advisors can't sell, but because advisors can't get in to see enough people — including people they know.

8: Does a growing prospect database increase sales for experienced agents? Yes! Many agents have little idea where next year's clients will emanate from. When you don't have a group of prospects with whom you employ an active strategy to personally circulate and heighten your professional reputation year in and year out, you will have no more security knowing where your new clients will evolve from in the future than what you have today. Without making a lifetime career commitment to a specific market where you can continuously build attraction to prospects, you will always have more sales insecurity than is necessary.

9: How can I get day-to-day acquaintances and social contacts, whether at my church or other organizations where I am involved, to agree to an appointment? Here is a simple and effective approach. When you suspect that a friend may be hesitant to accept an appointment request, start the conversation with the following: *"Just because we are friends doesn't mean you should be a client, but neither does it mean that you shouldn't be. And it certainly doesn't mean that I shouldn't put some information in your hands that gives you a better idea of where I am focusing my financial work. As a friend, I would like to buy you coffee or have lunch with you someday and give you a better idea of the work I am now doing. What's your schedule look like this week? Is Thursday a good day?"*

That simple phrase — *"Just because we are friends doesn't mean you should be a client, but neither does it mean that you shouldn't be"* — works magic when friends understand that you expect nothing, except a small amount of time to give them some information. Most will accept your appointment request.

10: Are demographic segments often confused as target markets? Many advisors mistake demographic segments of the general population for target markets. Demographic segment examples may include young married couples with children, small business owners, and families with income over $$$$. Demographic segments are appropriate for constructing a training program, but they don't provide a congregation of connected prospects that meets the three criteria for a target market:

- Common cause

- Personal appreciation for each other

- Structured time of assembly

Small Business Owners. You may want to focus your training on the needs of this market, but it is not a target market. Small business owners are a defined segment of prospects, appropriate for the product development department to assemble them as a focus group when looking for feedback on a new product, but they are too broad to fit the definition of a target market. Find a group of small business owners that has a commonality and meets every month. Now you have a target market where you can make an impact.

Young Married Couples with Children. Unless they are in the same church, synagogue or temple, they have few opportunities to regularly assemble as a group to build relationships, appreciation and camaraderie with each other. If there is no opportunity for you to consistently interact with this defined group each week or month, you can't deliver your reputation in a way that builds access to appointments.

Families with Income exceeding $$$$. This is not a target market. It's a demographic description of a population segment. It may help guide product and sales training, but it doesn't deliver you to any specific group of people where you can personally circulate, evolve a professional reputation, and endear yourself through continuous interactive connection.

11: Do advisors often mistake having a product focus as a target market? Asking an advisor about his target market produced this acclamation: *"I specialize in disability income insurance and finding people who need disability insurance."*

Whether or not you focus on long-term care, disability income, survivorship life, or qualified plans, it doesn't answer the question "Where is the group of people with whom you employ an active strategy to meet, circulate, and heighten your personal reputation month in and month out?"

12: Are some groups too loosely connected to be good target markets? Avoid targeting most groups that have entertainment, rather than a cause, as their focus. Such groups typically lack the ability to produce the results you would like to attain. You may belong to a wine tasting group, a running club, a sailing or ski club, but the infrequent group meetings are focused more on entertainment than a heartfelt cause. Most members attend these meetings sporadically, if at all, and are attracted to the group due to the entertainment activities planned and merchandise discounts. If you're interested in an entertainment-oriented group, join it, but don't consider it a serious target market. You may find a few prospects who become clients, but there will be little opportunity to make an ongoing impression with the majority of the members. The same warning applies to gym memberships and recreational athletic teams. A principle worth remembering is: the greater the heart-felt intensity of the cause, the greater the opportunity to become visible and appreciated within the group.

The 4 Sources for Prospects

Friends and Acquaintances

Referrals

Organizations

Events

A continually growing prospect database will influence your career success more than any other single component.

Everything else is minor.

PREFACE

Project 100 was my initiation to prospecting. While studying for my insurance license, I was asked to assemble a list of 100 people whose relationship with me spanned from close friends to casual acquaintances. Once contracted as a full-time agent, this would be my starting point to begin calling for appointments. These were to be my first prospects. Sound familiar?

The first few weeks proceeded nicely. My first twenty calls secured eight appointments. The other twelve wished me good luck while expressing that they were too busy now to meet. I later learned that this was really a "no," expressed kindly in an attempt to spare my feelings.

The second week produced similar results, with another four new appointments, but once I got past number thirty, the appointments became significantly more difficult. Many were old acquaintances I hadn't seen in years. Some were high school friends who had gone to different colleges and our paths had separated. Others were friends my wife had suggested, though I hardly knew them. Others were friends of my parents and sister.

After working past my initial good friends (my first thirty) and their few referrals, I concluded that the others on my list were no more receptive to an appointment request than if I were making a cold call. My Project 100 was turning out to be my Project 30. It wasn't nearly enough to sustain my career.

After my second week, in an attempt to keep me in front of new prospects, my manager acquired a list of upper-middle-income people within my zip code. These people owned homes with mortgages exceeding $150,000. Welcome Wagon leads became an additional source of names, comprised of people who were moving into the community, and weekly new births rounded out the quantity of prospects I needed to hopefully keep my sales activity moving.

Within a month, the realization hit. Between the mortgage lists, Welcome Wagon leads and new babies, my expectation of a fulfilling profession was gradually eroding. It was an unfriendly awakening. Cold calling was not very productive. It was painful. The rejections were often rude and abrupt — not something that would endear me to this career.

I learned quickly that prospecting was more than just having a name. I needed a more effective strategy that would create an ongoing source of appointments. I needed a market where I could somehow deliver my own professional reputation and create a compelling attraction. I didn't know the term, but without a target market with a strategically planned penetration plan, I was doomed.

My survival was not about selling; it was about prospecting. Real prospecting!

CHAPTER ONE

Rethinking Prospecting

(The following chapters reflect the prospecting experiences of Jeff. His prospecting focus made him a top advisor with his company his first year. His success continues to climb.)

My Project 200 was depleted. Between my friends and their few referrals, I had made thirteen sales and was now watching my activity drop to unacceptable lows. I knew that my initial 40 calls made from my list of 200 prospects represented about all the people who would realistically be receptive to an appointment. The others I barely knew or hadn't seen for years. I had to find a source for new prospects. It was time to figure out how to get my sales activity back up or face the reality that my career was winding down. I would be looking for a new career in the not-too-distant future.

The Chamber of Commerce monthly association luncheon would start in a few minutes. I had chosen the Chamber as one of two specific markets I wanted to target — not just briefly, but as a long-term career commitment. I wanted to imprint my reputation; become known and respected; and someday be seen as easily approachable — the "professional of choice" when it came to financial services for Chamber members. I had seen attorneys follow the same principle — picking a specific market and then building an enviable reputation. It worked miracles for their careers and I thought a specific focus might deliver the same for me.

I joined a table of five, taking the last remaining seat before the luncheon started. I intentionally picked a table with members I had never met. That's what prospecting is about — meeting new people and then having a strategy that eventually builds your reputation and a compelling attraction.

After about five minutes of introductions and light conversation, I extended my business card to the two people on my left and asked if I could have theirs in return. Here is what I said:

The Easy Business Card Request for Building Your Reputation

"Here's my business card. I would love to have one of yours. If I can get your information, I would like to place you in my database and, if it's okay, treat you as if you were one of my privileged clients for a few months. I'll send you the same monthly financial information that I send to my clients each month, with ideas on saving taxes, increasing after-tax wealth, insurance, and more. My clients really like these monthly financial briefs and I think you will too. In a few months, if something catches your attention, it might be a reason to grab lunch or coffee. Would that be okay?"

I had no more than received their business cards when I noticed that the three other people at the table were paying attention to our conversation. It was only natural to say to them, *"Oh, I'm sorry. I didn't want to interrupt your conversation but if you would like, give me your business cards and I will include you in my database as well. I think you will like the financial briefs that I send out to my clients each month. It will give you the opportunity to see the areas in which I focus my work and it will give me the opportunity to provide you with information on specific financial items if you ever see something of particular interest."* Without hesitation, three more business cards were handed my way.

If you're not adding fifteen new names a month to a prospect database, prospecting is not a priority.

Though I didn't need my new prospects' permission to place their e-mails in my database, I found that people appreciated my telling them what I intended to do. It also ensured that they would open my messages when they were sent.

This was my starting point to begin looking superior to the all-too-typical financial advisor who connects with clients once or twice a year, if at all. I quickly came to realize that if I kept focused on prospecting every day — *not* just once in a while — I could always find at least five people a week who could be added to my database. It wasn't a goal. It was more. It was an expectation I had of myself: add five new prospects every week to my database! It was a personal decision to give prospecting more than just lip service. It was my decision to never cold call again. This was a weekly action item that was in my control. Maybe it's time for you to make the same decision.

CHAPTER TWO

Never Lose a Prospect.
It's a Future CLIENT!

After attending the Chamber's association luncheon, I returned to my office and placed the five prospect names and their information into my database. My e-mail system (www.e-Relationship.com) was automated to send an introduction message to each of them immediately.

Dear Jack,

Economic and financial change happens at such a fast pace that it is often difficult to sort out the important issues that affect us directly. That is why I have just added your name to my address book. I will be sending you periodic e-briefs alerting you to up-to-date issues on security, protection, money and wealth — all areas in which I focus my work. And don't be surprised when you receive an occasional e-Holiday Card. I try to remember my clients and friends on days that are special and important.

Sincerely,
Jeff Smith
Financial Advisor

In addition, it would send out seven financial e-storyboards a year, a professionally written quarterly financial e-newsletter, four quarterly e-checklists, four e-holiday cards and an e-birthday card.

Without any effort on my part, my marketing system would communicate with every prospect twenty times per year, helping to build my reputation within the group. Additionally, I would see my fellow members numerous times a year while attending luncheons and activities within the association. I was committed to making this group a life-long market where I could build a compelling attraction. That would require more than just sending monthly information. It would require personal visibility and involvement, preferably every month. The sage advice of an old friend still rings through my ears today, *"An empty chair renders no attraction."*

I involved myself in the group and attended every meeting. Requesting a business card with an explanation of my intentions became my standard procedure with everyone. It was non-threatening, more often than not resulting in a thank-you. I discovered that this approach was applicable not only to new prospects, but also existing friends. Acquaintances I knew through church might be difficult to approach about an appointment, but they were very easy to ask for a business card. They always agreed to be included on a monthly e-mail.

The frequent e-mail connection allowed me to increase these friends' awareness of the type of work I was doing, give them an easy way to say "yes" to a monthly contact, and often, after the first or second mailing, provided me an opportunity to make a friendly phone call to gently coax them to grab a quick lunch. The worst that happened was being politely put off for a few more mailings. Eventually, the appointment was almost always assured, especially if I used the following words that turned almost any "No" for an appointment request into a "Not yet":

"Sometimes it's just not a good time to make an appointment. I understand that and I certainly respect it, but I hope it's okay if I keep you in my database (or add you to my database) and send you financial information throughout the year on ideas that may help you save taxes and increase after-tax wealth. It will give you a better understanding of where I focus my work and if something catches your attention, maybe we could grab coffee someday in the future. Is it okay if I keep you in my database and treat you as if you were one of my privileged clients for the next year or so?"

When building your reputation through monthly communication to 500-plus prospects, getting appointments becomes increasingly easy.

I now realized what the mantra "never lose a prospect" meant. Nearly all prospects will eventually agree to meet if you keep building the relationship by continually connecting with relevant and professional information. When their knowledge of you increases, your approachability is no longer a threat. Frequent connection matters. It is the only way to build a relationship, a professional reputation, and eventually become noted within your market.

CHAPTER THREE

From Prospect to Easy Appointment

When I initially joined the Chamber of Commerce, a number of my office colleagues informed me that they too had belonged to the organization at one time, but didn't feel it had yielded much in regard to sales. Sound familiar?

In reflecting on these individuals, I surmised they had never formulated a strategy to build a distinctive reputation in the Chamber. In all probability, they attended a limited number of meetings, sitting with familiar people instead of meeting new people when they did attend, and never became personally or meaningfully involved in the organization. Their objective was far more about them — what they could get — not about what they could give. They certainly never considered making the Chamber a lifetime career priority. My endeavor was going to be different. I was committed to making this successful.

I will admit that, after a few months of involvement with my targeted association, my appointment success was still not what I wanted. When I called people I had met and placed in my database, it often resulted in friendly conversations. But there were more "no" responses to my appointment requests than I desired. I needed something to help me transition from being someone they knew to someone they felt comfortable accepting an appointment request from. I needed something that caught their attention ... a unique identifier ... something that built a degree of attractive distinction and a sense of obligation.

At the next meeting of the Chamber, I arrived fifteen minutes early. Between the three or four arrival conversations I had and the six people I joined for lunch, I met seven new members that day and got business cards from all of them. I found that meeting five new people (my personal goal) and asking for a business card was no longer scary, but it did take discipline. I had to remind myself that this was *my* goal, not my manager's. It was about *my* career success, not his. It took a conscious commitment to stay focused each week on prospecting and asking for business cards, but I wasn't going to wimp out. I asked everywhere: church, Sunday school class, businesses I frequented, new people I met — and almost always experienced a welcomed response.

When I returned to my office that day, I was ready to implement my new strategy. After putting the seven new prospect names in my database, I inserted each business card into a plastic sleeve, pushed them through my business card laminator machine ($39.95 on eBay) and produced seven luggage tags, briefcase tags, or golf bag tags at ten cents each. Twenty seconds per tag was all it took and I was now ready to send the transformed business cards back to my new prospects, along with a personal letter.

George Davis
Davis Consulting, LLC
5350 Sunset Avenue
Anytown, CA 98111

Dear George,

I enjoyed meeting you today at the Chamber of
Commerce luncheon and hope that we will have
a chance to become more acquainted sometime
in the future.

You have probably noticed that I am returning your
business card. After inserting your information into my
client database, so I could fulfill my promise of treating
you as a privileged client for a year, I laminated it
for your use as a luggage, golf bag or briefcase tag.
My clients always enjoy these and I thought you
might find a use for this one.

Over the next few months, please allow me to e-mail
some periodic messages on areas in which I focus
my work — reducing taxes and increasing after-tax
wealth. Many clients find these messages useful in strat-
egizing their own financial objectives throughout the
year, and I am confident you will experience the same.

When your schedule permits, let's grab a quick lunch.
If you need a few more luggage tags laminated, let me
know. I would be glad to give you a set for your next
travel plans.

Sincerely,

Jeff Smith, Financial Advisor

Three days after sending the letter and business card tag, I made a phone call.

"*Hello* (name). *This is* (agent name). *I was calling to see if you received my letter with your business card that I returned — the one that I laminated into a luggage tag. Did you get it?*"

That was all there was to it! The phone response always started with a surprised "thank you!" and progressed from there.

Letting them know that I did this a lot for my clients, I would offer to laminate a few more business cards in the event they were planning a vacation or needed one for a golf bag. I would then suggest that we get together someday for coffee or lunch and let me put some information in their hands as to areas that I focused my financial work. That information, along with the occasional e-mail updates I was planning to send, would give them a start to determine in the future if I could help them in any way. Suggesting a specific day and time for lunch or coffee, letting them know this was not a sales pitch, and encouraging them to bring a few more business cards for me to laminate almost always got a positive response.

What consistent action have you embraced that defines you as more likeable and distinctly different from the competition?

My appointment ratio with this approach soared. Between adding new people to my prospect database, treating them like they were already privileged clients, and then creating the special laminated business card tags for them, I found that responses to my appointment requests were astoundingly better than my old traditional approach.

Why was this approach so successful? Because returning a business card as a luggage tag is remarkable, relevant, and personal. Those are the three measurements for determining if an activity will be regarded as a unique identifier. If so, it has the ability to distinguish you from the expected norm and create a feeling of reciprocation.

- **Remarkable**. No one has ever returned your business card!

- **Relevant**. The recipients know immediately where they will use their laminated tags.

- **Personal**. It was made just for them. It's not a logo-stamped company pen or magnetic calendar intended for the masses. Their personal business card, now turned into a luggage tag, won't get thrown away. It took thoughtfulness and personal time and that deserves a thank-you — a simple act of reciprocation. I can't tell you how many thank-you's I receive every month. It never stops and it never gets old.

(Don't ever substitute a company logo luggage tag holder to insert the person's business card. That turns this great idea into an advertisement gimmick. It is no longer personal! The benefit is perceived as yours, not theirs!)

Getting Started with Luggage Tags

You can purchase luggage tag sleeves at www. factory-express.com under Laminating Supplies, (item number POUC111). It's a "Luggage Tag W/ Slot" priced at $7 for 100. Plastic luggage tag loops (POUC905) are also located under Laminating Supplies, priced at $9 for 100. If purchasing a luggage tag laminator, consider the GBC HeatSeal H110 Pouch Laminator (E-LAM5355), currently priced around $50.

CHAPTER
FOUR

Transitioning Friends to Easy Appointments

Have you ever felt that it was sometimes harder to get a friend to accept an appointment than it was a cold prospect? I have. Maybe my friends felt like they would be obligated to buy. Maybe they felt that since they knew me, I would apply more sales pressure. I am not sure what it was, but I eventually found the formula to ask a friend for an appointment.

The Appointment Request to a Friend

"Jack, just because we're friends doesn't mean that you should be my client, but neither does it mean that you shouldn't be. And it certainly doesn't mean that I shouldn't put some information in your hands that gives you a better idea of where I am focusing my financial work. I would like to buy you coffee or have lunch with you someday and give you a better idea of the work I am now doing. What's your schedule look like this week? Is Thursday a good day?"

That simple phrase — *"Just because we're friends doesn't mean that you should be my client, but neither does it mean that you shouldn't be"* — seemed to work magic. They understood that I expected nothing except a small amount of time to give them some information. Friendship was more important and I assured them that was the case.

The Business Card Request

If a friend hesitated at all to my appointment request, I would then say:

"Jack, give me your business card. I'm going to at least put you in my database and send you occasional financial e-briefs and financial newsletters that you may find valuable. As a friend, the least I can do is to treat you like a privileged client and give you a better idea of the financial area in which I focus my business. If you like it or in the future find an item that grabs your interest, we can grab lunch at that time."

Without hesitation, the business card would be handed over. If they didn't have a business card available, I would ask for an e-mail address, assuring them that they would enjoy the communication every month.

Whether or not a friend agrees to your first request for an appointment is immaterial. Getting a new client is often about taking one step forward. Any friend will agree to being treated as a privileged client. Include them in your database and start connecting every month to heighten your professional relevance. Your consistent connection will raise your reputation above the competition and pave the way for an eventual appointment.

CHAPTER FIVE

Embracing My Natural Market

All of us have a natural market. It may be your church or synagogue, a civic club, country club, a swim club, parents whose children play on your child's Little League baseball or soccer team, fellow coaches involved with you in a city's recreational coaching program, fellow actors who participate in community theatre productions, fellow teammates involved in your city tennis league, etc.

Everyone in your natural market should be considered legitimate prospects. If you don't make them your prospects, someone else will. Friends who know you, even casually, would rather do business with you than a stranger. But if you don't treat them as privileged clients by sending monthly information on financial topics as a strategy to court them into client status, someone else will. You lose. Get it?

If you can't identify at least 500 prospects to place in a database (friends, social acquaintances and organizations you're connected to), then you're not serious about prospecting.

Your job is to continually identify new prospects and create a courting strategy. With a little effort, anyone can assimilate a database of at least 500 future clients (1,000 is better) within thirty days and then add fifteen each month.

You may want to begin your prospecting focus by considering the following ten ideas for assembling a prospect database.

1: Friends and Acquaintances

Who do you already know? Your friends and casual acquaintances should be your future clients. All of them! Add them to your database now. Stop being hesitant about working with friends. Even if they won't meet with you at this time, they will agree to let you send e-mail information throughout the year. The constant connection makes a huge impact and eventually creates a sense of obligation. Consistent connection magnifies your professional reputation and quickly positions you as superior to most of the competition. When that occurs, asking for an appointment becomes significantly more comfortable for both you and the prospect.

2: Religious Affiliation

If you attend a church, synagogue or temple, quit being shy. Get the names of those whom you would like as clients and place them in a database. They will appreciate the monthly informational mailings and learning more about you. Eventually, it becomes only natural for them to meet with you and become your newest clients.

3: Country Club, Swim Club, Recreational Club

If you belong to a country club or swim club, put the membership list in your database. You don't need to e-mail-blitz the entire group; send information to 100 contacts one week and another group of contacts in two weeks. Those who have no interest will opt out. The others will be great future clients and receptive to future mailings. They will now know more about you when you ask for an appointment.

4: Civic Club

Join a civic club that has active members and is an adequate size (at least 150). Most successful agents are involved in a civic group. Put the names of every member in your database and start building your reputation and their knowledge of the areas in which you focus your business.

5: Occupational Association

Find one occupational organization (minimum size 300) where you would like to be recognized eventually as the financial service professional of choice. Every industry has a supporting organization — among them home builders, restaurant owners, landscapers, chiropractors, HVAC contractors, importers/exporters, and professional women in construction. Anyone can join an occupational association as an ancillary member and be welcomed if you support members in the organization with services they want and need — such as retirement planning, life insurance, group health, LTC, etc. Over 60% of every occupational association is comprised of ancillary members, such as bank executives who are required by their bank to attend every monthly meeting, participate in golf outings and be involved in fund-raisers. It is part of their corporate business strategy to establish friendships leading to new business. Follow their example.

Don't wait to become an experienced veteran agent to join. Join as a young agent, get involved, attend meetings and add value. It's a sure way to build your career.

6: Join a Large General Business Association

Join the Chamber of Commerce, NAWBO (National Association of Women Business Owners), Human Resource Association (SPHR, SHRM), Young Entrepreneurs Association, or a general business association that has a large membership (over 300) and a regularly scheduled luncheon meeting each month. These are easy places to meet people who are building successful careers. Add the members to your database. After a few mailings, they will recognize your name when you call or when you meet them at luncheons and group functions. There is a cumulative effect as the months and years progress. In particular, joining an HR association will give you access to many businesses and an opportunity to become the director's professional of choice for 401(k) rollouts at terminations and retirements. Build your reputation within one of these groups and your sales will be positively affected for years to come.

7: Charity

Get active with a local charity that you have a genuine interest in and then volunteer for the fund-raising committee. Call on one business owner a week to explain your organization's cause and ask for a contribution. First, you will be a hero to the charity. Second, if you had a good meeting, before leaving explain your business focus and ask if you could add him or her to your database with the intention of sending occasional items of financial interest. Call back in a few weeks and schedule lunch. Do this four times a month and, more than likely, you have just secured two new future clients, as well as served a worthy cause. You will catapult your reputation and career in more ways than you can imagine. Guaranteed!

If you don't want to fund-raise for a charity, join the Chamber of Commerce and volunteer as an Appreciation Ambassador. Each month, you can contact four longtime members (of at least 10 years), take them a new information packet to remind them of the organization's value, and present them at the same time with a dozen dough-nuts as a gesture of thanks. (Numerous doughnut chains are happy to provide the doughnuts for free.) After reviewing the Chamber information packet with the business owners, ask if you can add them to your business database and stay in touch with occasional e-information on financial ideas. This is an easy way to meet business people in a very non-self-serving way. For more info on the program, call Identity Branding at 800-851-8169.

8: Add 15 New Prospects Each and Every Month

Commit to adding fifteen new prospects every month to your database — people you meet, fellow club members, church acquaintances, friends you have overlooked, people you did business with this month, referrals who said "no" to an appointment request. If you don't make a monthly habit of identifying and adding fifteen prospects to your database each month, you aren't paying attention and prospecting is not a priority. It is time for you to believe that every prospect is a future client. Every prospect will need a product that you offer in the next five years and, if you stay connected, you create tremendous preference and emotional safety. The more prospects you stay consistently connected with, the greater the success you will experience in your career.

9: Referrals

Get referrals. Not just occasionally but as a regular practice. Read the book *Referrals Made Easy ... it's just NOT that hard!* (Robert Krumroy, 2011). Most clients will give you two referrals even if your "asking" technique needs some tweaking. Ask at the end of the sale ... not at delivery. If you're not getting referrals, it's because you're wimping out. Stop being a wimp!

10: Believe that EVERY Prospect Is a Future Client

Print out the phrase "Every prospect is a future client" and tape it to your desk, on your bathroom mirror, and in your car. When you start to internalize this belief, you will realize that adding fifteen names to your prospect database every month may have more value than the eight sales you made this month. Yes ... *every prospect* is a future client. Build your database with fifteen new prospects every month and three years from now your business will be magnificent. *You* will be a super producer with a major reputation!

Every prospect is a future client! Treat each one of them like that and your business will soar.

CHAPTER SIX

What Are the Best Target Markets?

Successfully delivering oneself to a target market is the most important activity you can do to build ongoing high-level sales success and career fulfillment. Without a lifetime commitment to being meaningfully involved with a target market of significant size, you will endure prospecting challenges throughout your career.

Target markets that yield the greatest results in appointments and sales are made up of people who share three criteria:

- A common cause (the more intense the cause, the better the group)

- A personal appreciation for each other (especially those who are actively involved)

- A regularly structured meeting time (at least once a month) to support their cause or life value — personal or business

Leaving out even one of the three components will have a huge negative effect on your ability to build a compelling attraction within a segment of targeted prospects. And there is one additional component that is critical to your selection:

You need to have a personal appreciation for the group and affection for the people in the group, and you need to believe in the cause they support.

Finding a specific group that appeals to you as a possible target market may be the result of the cause, the overall personality of the membership, or acceptance into the group. If you don't currently have access to a personal target market, consider first the professions or affiliations of your father, mother and siblings. Does an association support their occupation? You may feel very comfortable focusing your career within their group, already having a natural understanding and appreciation for the profession and a family advocate who supports your entry.

Consider close friends who may belong to an occupational association, such as the home builders association, pest control association, chiropractic association, etc. Could they help deliver you to a target market? What about friends who belong to a civic organization — Kiwanis, Rotary, Lion's Club, etc. — or others who may belong to the Young Entrepreneurs Association, National Association of Women Business Owners (NAWBO), or the Hispanic Chamber?

Tell your friends, clients and centers of influence that you are narrowing your business focus and use the following approach:

Asking Friends to Introduce You to their Organization

"(Name), *I am going to ask you for your opinion about the* (group) *you're involved with. I am considering narrowing my business focus to specifically serve two or three groups. In other words, I would like to build a reputation as a specialist to a specific group of clients. I am looking for maybe two groups that might be a good match and organizations that I can really get involved with. I wondered what your thoughts were about your organization. I also wondered if you think it would be appropriate to take me to a meeting sometime to let me evaluate the potential."*

Asking a friend to help you consider his or her group as a potential focus for your business usually invokes an enthusiastic invitation to the next meeting along with strong encouragement that the organization may be a great fit for your efforts. Your friend's pride in the group will be very evident, and at the next luncheon meeting, you will be introduced to everyone. It's a tremendous advantage to have a natural champion help you assimilate into a group as you begin a lifetime career focus.

Do Some Target Market Research

If you are just starting your search for a target market, one that attracts your interest and is large enough to be a major source of ongoing prospects, here is how to start.

1: Go to Google and type in the name of your city and the word Association. For additional selections, repeat the process but type in the words Membership Organizations.

2: Look at associations that attract your interest.

3: Find associations with at least 200 members, which is minimal. If membership size is not publicized, click on the join button. Many organizations will show their size in the join section.

4: Make sure the organization holds regular meetings.

5: Plan to attend the next meeting as a guest to determine if the group's a good fit for you.

Here are some associations and organizations in different parts of the country that could be excellent target markets. Similar groups exist in your community.

Southern Arizona Black Chamber of Commerce
Meeting Frequency: Monthly +
Member Size: 283
Membership Cost: $150

NAWBO (National Association of Women Business Owners)
Meeting Frequency: Monthly +
Membership Size: 204
Membership Cost: $275

Northern Pima Arizona Chamber of Commerce
Meeting Frequency: Monthly +
Member Size: 400+
Membership Cost: $225

Tucson Utility Contractors Association
Meeting Frequency: Monthly +
Member Size: 116 (Utility contractors
   and earth movers)
Membership Cost: Call for information.

Seattle Active Christians
Meeting Frequency: Monthly +
Membership Size: 737
Membership Cost: $0

Downtown Seattle Association

Meeting Frequency: Monthly +
Member Size: 641
Membership Cost: $525

Greater Seattle Business Association (LGBT)

Meeting Frequency: Monthly
Member Size: 1,000+
Membership Cost: $100

Seattle Women's Business Exchange

Meeting Frequency: Monthly
Member Size: 200
Membership Cost: $125

North Carolina World Trade Association

Meeting Frequency: Monthly +
Member Size: 1,000+
Membership Cost: $70 - $350

SPHR (HR Association)

Meeting Frequency: Monthly
Member Size: 800+
Membership Cost: $250

Charlotte Restaurant Association

Meeting Frequency: Monthly
Member Size: large (not specified except
   to members)
Membership Cost: $249

Kiwanis Club of Charlotte

Meeting Frequency: Weekly
Member Size: 500+
Membership Cost: not specified,
   approximately $300

Greensboro Home Builders Association
Meeting Frequency: Monthly
Member Size: 731
Membership Cost: $470

High Point Human Resource Association (SHRM)
Meeting Frequency: Monthly
Member Size: 200+
Membership Cost: $140

Dallas Building Owners and Managers Association (BOMA)
Meeting Frequency: Monthly
Member Size: 1,000+
Membership Cost: $250

Dallas Chapter – National Association of Women in Construction
Meeting Frequency: Monthly
Member Size: 400+
Membership Cost: $217

Dallas NAWBO (National Association of Women Business Owners)
Meeting Frequency: Monthly
Member Size: 600+
Membership Cost: $175

Greater San Antonio Builders Association
Meeting Frequency: Monthly
Member Size: 500+
Membership Cost: $400

San Antonio Manufacturers Association
Meeting Frequency: Monthly
Member Size: 450+
Membership Cost: $250+

Christian Women's Small Business Association
Meeting Frequency: Monthly
Member Size: 498
Membership Cost: Call for information.

Rotary Club of San Antonio
Meeting Frequency: Weekly
Member Size: 514
Membership Cost: $300+

Greater Atlanta Home Builders Association
Meeting Frequency: Monthly
Member Size: 1,023
Membership Cost: $400

Southern Nursery Association
Meeting Frequency: Monthly
Member Size: 1,600+
Membership Cost: Call for information.

CHAPTER SEVEN

Event Prospecting

Remember that there are only four sources for meeting and finding new prospects in today's market: Friends and Acquaintances, Referrals, Organizations, and Events. As we get older, our social circles don't normally expand. They actually begin to contract. We find ourselves focused on family, children, grandchildren and a few close friends. If we don't consciously extend ourselves to organizations and become involved in events, access to new prospects will eventually contract.

We all have naturally occurring events in our day-to-day lives that can become sources for attracting new prospects, but only if the strategy for attraction is:

• Relevant

• Remarkable

• Personally (not financially) Beneficial

On the following pages are three prime examples of event prospecting.

Church/Synagogue/Temple Picnic Photo Album Event

Does your church or place of worship have a summer picnic? Volunteer to take photos of the event, sending the photo album to the entire congregation, even those who are not present. Don't do it just once. Make a personal commitment to do it every year. When sending the photo album, remark in the personal message to each recipient what a great time it was and encourage everyone to attend the fall cleanup day scheduled in September or the next event that the church has planned. Your place of worship will appreciate the announcement and the encouragement to attend the next event.

People love to see pictures of themselves, and as the photographer you have just moved up a rung on the ladder of trust and approachability. Your personal involvement in the lives of those who share your church connection makes you distinctly different and appreciated. Your actions will be viewed as relevant, remarkable, and personal.

Now that you have everyone's e-mail address, begin building your professional reputation by connecting with informational e-mailing on financial issues, mixed with e-holiday cards and e-newsletters throughout the year. You will be pleasantly surprised how easily this will open the door to appointments with people who have a new level of knowledge about you and an appreciation for your unique involvement in their lives.

The Business Owner's Expo Event

Would you like to easily create an elevated appreciation of yourself among a number of business owner prospects? It will make a big difference when asking for an interview. Here's how. Contact your local Chamber of Commerce or convention center to get the date of the next annual business expo or home show. Purchase a ticket to the event — not a booth. Take a digital camera and approach the local business owners at each booth by handing them your business card. Here is what you should say:

The Trade Show Approach

"My name is _____ and I specialize in working with small-business owners here in _____ on retirement plans, insurance, and employee benefits (or ... selective business owner perks that the business can pay for instead of you paying out-of-pocket). However, even though that's my area of focus, I am not here to talk about financial services or to ask for an appointment. That might be the highlight of your day — a financial guy not asking for an appointment?! (Wait for a smile or chuckle.) *What I am doing here today is taking pictures of all of the booths so that we can provide a copy of the exhibit hall's photo album to every owner. That way they can see what others did that might be adaptable next year and help increase their booth's attraction. My clients always like this, but this year I am providing a copy of the photo album for everyone. Can I get your picture here in the booth and then I will send you a copy of the album in the next two days. Would that be okay?"*

Send the e-photo album within two to five days and then send a financial e-storyboard within a week. You will be surprised at the number of business owners who will request information for details on retirement issues, insurance, etc. You have just created an event that was remarkable, relevant and personally beneficial. That's the first ingredient in building a professional reputation that elevates you above what they have previously experienced in the financial service industry. You offered to "give" first without trying to "get," and that is unique.

Golf Tournament Opportunities

Organizations of all stripes hold golf tournaments for members and guests, with weekday events attracting mostly business owners and affluent individuals. Don't overlook your church, synagogue, temple, civic club, or favorite charity and when you call the golf course, inquire about occupational groups, such as dental and home builder associations. Just call any private or public golf course and ask who is looking for hole sponsors for this summer's golf tournaments. The response will be enthusiastic and loaded with choices. Average hole sponsorships (not playing) typically range from $100 to $200, and you should expect to meet 75 to 125 new prospects.

Do not sign up to play. Instead, sponsor the watering hole (#9). That's the hole that provides free beer and soft drinks to the golfers. Take a photo of each foursome and sponsor a longest-drive marshmallow contest while they're waiting for the foursome in front to get far enough away to tee off. Provide each golfer with two marshmallows and say that the longest marshmallow drive wins a car. Have a matchbox car in your pocket and when the foursome has finished hitting the marshmallows, pull out the car and present it to the winner.

Make sure you take a photo of the winner with the other three golfers standing behind him or her. Use different style matchbox cars (89 cents) and watch as the golfers trade cars at the end of the event. It will become iconic and you will be remembered and appreciated.

Your job is to become every prospect's second-favorite financial service provider. Once accomplished, they are *your* future clients – *guaranteed*!

Make sure to request a business card from each golfer, in order to share photos of the event. For golfers who don't have business cards, have a legal pad or index card handy so they can print their names and e-mail addresses. If you use pre-printed cards, you can also collect birth dates and company names. Tell the golfers you will include them on your monthly e-briefs about financial issues, which often provide tips on retirement issues, saving taxes and increasing after-tax income, your particular areas of focus. Many will engage you in conversation on the spot, making it very evident which of them might be your easiest prospects to approach for an appointment.

Don't forget to laminate the business cards into luggage tags and mail them to the golfers. Follow up with a phone call in three days and watch how easy it is to open the door for an appointment. Send the golf photo album within five days, however, or your efforts will be wasted.

There are numerous events in your community that provide opportunities for meeting new prospects. You can find more than twenty examples in the book *Please...Make ME a little bit FAMOUS!* The point to remember is: It doesn't matter what you choose to do; it only matters that you do something.

Without consciously involving yourself in organizations and events, your prospecting will eventually wither and so will your growth in income and career satisfaction. Prospecting is not a skill for just the new advisor; it is a skill for every advisor and it needs to continue forever. If you're not adding fifteen new names to a prospect database each month, you're not prospecting. Eventually, that will prove to be a fatal mistake.

CHAPTER EIGHT

Making a Lifetime Career Commitment to Prospecting

Everyone acknowledges that the hardest part of a financial service career is prospecting, yet few give it the attention it deserves. If you don't have a prospect database that grows steadily month after month, your claim that prospecting is a priority is delusional.

Have you now selected a target market in order to get more prospects? Don't! Select a target market in order to make a lifetime career commitment. The difference is more than words; the difference results in a far superior outcome!

As we have shown, advisors who make a lifetime career commitment to a specific group or groups excel in sales, income, and career satisfaction. They understand that today's prospects need to do more than just meet you — they need to experience you — and that's the key to achieving big results.

Twenty years ago, focusing on a target market for the purpose of getting new prospects worked. Today's prospect wants more personal interaction (non-business), more assurance of your genuineness and, finally, they want proof that your business distinction is relevant and distinct as compared to what they consider to be the typical competition.

We have all encountered the agent who joins an organization and then laments about minimal appointments and lack of additional sales. Yet there are thousands of examples of agents who become well recognized in organizations, attain almost exclusive dominance as the preferred financial advisor and have great sales results. The distinction between the two outcomes occurs not because of their choice of target markets but the difference in their commitment to give value and deliver meaningful involvement to the group.

Prospecting is not about selecting a group to get clients from; it is about selecting a group to whom you are willing to give value to.

It's now time for you to select your target market(s) where you can make a lifetime career commitment. The sales results will appear when the membership sees the value delivered.

CHAPTER NINE

Social Media – Image Enhancement, Sales, Referrals

This prospecting book would not be complete without a brief comment on the value of social media as it pertains to prospecting. When you expose Twitter, LinkedIn, and Facebook friends to posts that mention your accomplishments, industry/company awards, and designation achievements or you take the time to include a link to a financial services article, it may help build your business reputation and personal image. However, the passivity of social media is not a substitute for implementing a proactive target marketing strategy or for building a prospect database of significant size — and then frequently communicating with those prospects in order to establish a superior personal image.

When looking for prospects whom you would like to eventually turn into clients, don't forget that the names in your social media address book can be exported to your prospect database.

When using social media, pay attention to potential sales opportunities. By staying alert, you can identify life events that might trigger a selling opportunity, such as the birth of a child, a child's college graduation, marriage, a new home, a new job, retirement. All of these present opportunities to make contact and quite possibly secure an appointment. And don't forget that when your clients are members of Facebook, LinkedIn, Twitter, or other social media, you can search for people who may work in their companies or be involved in the same activities as they are. Identifying the names to the client is a great way to stimulate a referral discussion and, if appropriate, ask for an introduction.

In summary, social media should not be considered a primary lead-generation program that you can depend on to build your financial services business. It is, however, a growing tool that can be very helpful for enhancing your image and identifying selling and referral opportunities that previously might have gone unnoticed.

EPILOGUE

It is now up to you.

There is nothing that will impact your success more than prospecting.

There is nothing more tragic than allowing prospects to drop through the cracks.

There is no elongated course on prospecting that is going to provide the "little secret" we left out.

There is no coaching that is going to substitute for prospecting.

There is no administrative assistant who is going to do prospecting for you.

There is no alternative for your getting personally involved.

There is no more.

It is all about you.

When you decide you want a higher level of success, easier appointments and greater career satisfaction, it's time to make prospecting — *real prospecting* — your number one priority.

And remember ... *it's just NOT that hard!*

Competitive products are no longer unique. Advanced support is not a differentiator. Hope is not a strategy.

Take a day to build an attraction strategy, be consistent in implementation, and watch your reputation soar above the norm.

It is the wise business person who dares to open his or her mind to new ways of capturing clients and outperforming the competition.

Allow me to introduce you to a powerful set of programs and tools created by Identity Branding that will give you the inspiration, motivation and skills to be consistently successful.

Please...Make ME a little bit FAMOUS!
A Must Read!

In this book, Robert offers a cutting-edge approach to creating prospect attraction in today's skeptical marketplace. His first book, Identity Branding—Creating Prospect Attraction, was reprinted four times and is still used in study groups all over America. This new book takes the practical advice even further. It has over 180 pages describing in  detail the newest prospect attraction strategies — examples that show sales professionals how to open doors to desirable prospects and make themselves a little bit FAMOUS in their local communities.

Please...Make ME a little Bit FAMOUS!
Complete Marketing Kit

Robert Krumroy's acclaimed financial industry book Please...Make ME a little bit FAMOUS is now available on CD, with 21 mini-marketing booklets as a bonus. This marketing kit is a must-have if you want to build dominant recognition in your local community. Each of the booklets reveals an awareness strategy used by super achievers to build recognition, surprise,  delight and appreciation with prospects and clients. Just choose or adapt the strategy that fits your personality and market. All of the information you need to implement a strategy (including sample letters and order forms) are included here. It's an unbeatable way to learn how to open doors in your market.

Identity Branding Revisited—
Creating Prospect Attraction
For Financial Planners and Insurance Agents

Already in its fourth printing, this is the most talked about marketing book in the financial industry. Within 9 months of being released, a second printing was required. Over 200 pages that give you the secrets to creating a visible differentiation in the marketplace; a client perception of superior value; a consumer preference for you. Don't miss this powerful book.

Brilliant Strategies and Fatal Blunders
This book is a must read!

Working hard, providing a quality product or being personally determined to "gut it out" until people recognize your expertise and give you their business no longer attains high-level success. High-level success requires critical thinking; building visible market differentiation; and then outclassing the competition. This book identifies the brilliant strategies used by professionals, service companies and retail establishments to

do just that ... beat the competition and thrive. But caution, the fatal blunders are practically invisible and almost always terminal. If you want to survive and thrive, read this book.

It's NOT About Luck!

Impression management is the new skill for creating prospect attraction and solving your advisor's appointment activity challenge. As a manager, nothing will cause greater appointment and production increases than directing your advisors in building effective prospect-attraction strategies. When done correctly, clients will increase their loyalty and prospects will enthusiastically agree to appointments with your advisors, concluding that they are remarkable and far superior to the competition. Apply this new skill and watch your advisor's activity, production, retention, recruiting and your firm's reputation soar to new heights.

The Prospect Relationship Ladder

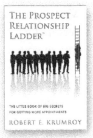

Old traditional methods of "getting in" don't work — not like they once did; even better phone approaches produce minimal improvements. Today's methods and systems for gaining prospect access are new and must be learned. Helping your prospect climb the Relationship Ladder to the Emotional Safety Rung will cause your appointment success to soar ... as well as significantly impact your sales! Read this book.

Sell the Problem
This book is a must read!

Have you missed a sale lately? Did you do a poor job presenting your solution ... or the problem? Most advisors don't sell the problem adequately before attempting to sell their solution. The prospect must buy the cost of the problem first! Learn to sell the pain, the loss and the unwanted consequences of the problem and you will have an easy time selling the solution.

Referrals Made Easy

Learning to get referrals doesn't require spending a fortune on an expensive course. It doesn't require learning a myriad of replies to overcome objections. It doesn't require you to watch multiple videos for weeks on end. It doesn't require you to join a weekly peer group that promises to shame you into performing. This book debunks the mystery that getting referrals is hard. *It's not!* Learn the three simple components and then ... don't wimp out. Get into the referral game and do it now!

Marketing Booklets

Every advisor has a "getting in" problem in today's environment. Prospects, even referrals, are hesitant to say "yes" to an appointment request. The bottom line is if you want to solve the "getting in" problem, you must apply a "getting in" solution. Separating you from the competition requires differentiation and high-level consistent visibility. Consistent visibility is the hallmark of attraction. Heightening awareness of you and your differentiated business reputation is critical for gaining attraction. Frequent visibility is imperative if you expect the majority of your appointment requests to be accepted. Robert Krumroy, President of Identity Branding/e-Relationship™, has developed Creating Prospect Approachability Booklets, which provide ideas that produce exceptional results.

Prospecting Made Easy
Keynote Speeches & Workshops

Most Difficult Part of Selling Life Insurance (Top 4 Answers):
2011, LIMRA STUDY COMPLETED BY 2,200 AGENTS

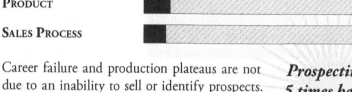

PROSPECTING — 52%

REGULATORY PRESSURES — 14%

PRODUCT — 12%

SALES PROCESS — 10%

Career failure and production plateaus are not due to an inability to sell or identify prospects. They are the result of an inability to create prospect access. The old, traditional approach is not the solution. It's no longer about finding people who need your product and can afford to pay for it. The rules have changed. Prospecting in today's market requires knowing how to build a compelling attraction to people who can and will become your clients.

Prospecting is 5 times harder than sales!

If you want to increase retention and production, it's time to talk prospecting!

HERE IS WHAT YOU WILL LEARN:

- *How to transition friends and acquaintances to guaranteed appointments*

- *Making Referrals Easy — It's just NOT that hard!*

- *How you can build access to hesitant prospects*

- *How to look superior in comparison to the typical competition*

- *Knowing the markets with the best sales potential for you*

e-relationship™

The number-one e-connection tool in the financial industry!

Consistent connection is one of the mainstays of being a highly successful financial advisor. Our e-Relationship™ automated e-mail program makes it delightfully easy to keep in touch with every prospect and client in your database. Send holiday e-cards, e-birthday wishes, e-newsletters and more throughout the year. Also choose from 125 prepackaged financial e-briefs. Each message is personalized and sent one at a time—no multiple-name mailing list is ever seen by your recipients.

www.e-relationship.com

PLEASE PROVIDE INFORMATION ON:

❏ Prospect Attraction Workshops ❏ Speaking Engagements

BOOKS:

❏ *Prospecting Made Easy* .... $7^{95} _____
❏ *Referrals Made Easy* .... $7^{95} _____
❏ *Sell the Problem — The Prospect Will Beg For a Solution!* ..... $9^{95} _____
❏ *The Prospect Relationship Ladder* .... $16^{95} _____
❏ *Please...Make ME a little bit FAMOUS!* .... $24^{95} _____
❏ *Please...Make ME a little bit FAMOUS! Audio Version* ..... $39^{95} _____
❏ *Identity Branding — Revisited* .... $19^{95} _____
❏ *Brilliant Strategies and Fatal Blunders* .... $18^{95} _____
❏ *It's NOT About Luck!* (Manager Book) .... $39^{95} _____

MARKETING KIT:

❏ *Please...Make ME a little bit FAMOUS!*
Complete Marketing Kit .... $99^{95} _____
(Includes 21 Idea Booklets & *Please...Make ME a little bit FAMOUS!* Audio Book)

PAYMENT INFORMATION

Name _____ Phone Number _____

Company _____

E-mail Address _____

Office Mailing Address _____

City _____ State _____ Zip Code _____

Card Number _____ Expiration Date _____

Signature _____

❏ AMEX ❏ MasterCard ❏ VISA ❏ Discover ❏ Invoice Me

NOTE: Additional S/H charges will apply.

Fax to 336-303-7318

Identity Branding, Inc.
3300 Battleground Avenue, Suite 250, Greensboro, NC 27410
www.identitybranding.com / www.e-relationship.com
800-851-8169

"Relevant and remarkable! Use a third of the ideas in this book and success is all but guaranteed."

Donald Molineu, Jr.
FICF, LLIF, South Carolina State Manager
WOODMEN OF THE WORLD

"Krumroy has simplified another complex topic. New agents can easily grasp it and experienced advisors can adapt the straightforward strategies to reinvigorate their practices! A must read!"

Daniel Shanahan
Agency Manager
GUARDIAN LIFE INSURANCE CO. OF AMERICA

"Bob's new book absolutely nails prospecting in these changing times — the best I've seen published in my 29 years. It's mandatory reading for all new recruits, if not every advisor on our team!"

Desi P. Doise
FICF, CLU, LLIF, State Manager — Louisiana
WOODMEN OF THE WORLD

"Bob has once again boiled down a very intimidating and complex process to an easy-to-understand and duplicatable process."

Mickey Moore
CLU, ChFC, Senior VP, Career Distribution
AVIVA USA

"Being brilliant at the basic skills is critical to being successful in our business, and prospecting is at the foundation of those skills. This book will ensure your prospecting funnel is always full."

Abram M. Gibbons
LUTCF, VP Training & Development
GUARDIAN

"Prospecting Made Easy is yet another powerful book with easy-to-use strategies that will help you reach new heights of success. Every advisor should read and implement the information. Every firm should promote it. Thank you, Bob, for another great resource."

Edward G. Deutschlander
CLU, CLF, CEO Elect
NORTH STAR RESOURCE GROUP